Lineage of the Jedi

*The Jedi Training Manual:
One Spirit Medicine to Activate the Light Body
and Heal the Planet*

Jesse Adam Hollis

Copyright © 2024

All rights reserved.

All rights reserved. No part of this publication may be reproduced, distributed, or transmitted in any form or by any means, including photocopying, recording, or other electronic or mechanical methods, without the author's prior written permission, except in the case of brief quotations embodied in critical reviews and certain other non-commercial uses permitted by copyright law. For permission requests, please get in touch with the author.

Contents

Dedication i
Acknowledgements i
About the Author iii
Introduction 1
Chapter 1: The Jedi 4
Chapter 2: History Of This Planet 7
Chapter 3: The Force 10
Chapter 4: The Light Side Vs. The Dark Side 14
Chapter 5: Jedi Vs. Sith 16
Chapter 6: In Order To Find Enlightenment: Chop Wood, Cook Food And Carry Water 18
Chapter 7: The Medicine Wheel & Creating Sacred Space 22
Chapter 9: Lucid Dreaming 27
Chapter 10: Kundalini Awakening 31
Chapter 11: The Luminous Energy Field 33
Chapter 12: The Rainbow Body 34
Chapter 13: The Higher Self 36
Chapter 14: The Ego 38
Chapter 15: Chakras & Meridians 40
Chapter 16: Gaining Focus And Building One Pointed Force Awareness 49
Chapter 17: Oneness, Samadhi And Resonance: Light Body Activation 52
Chapter 18: The Future Planetary Jedi Order 55
Chapter 19: Fear & The Shadow 57
Chapter 20: Psychic Attack & Defensive Practices 60
Chapter 21: Trauma & Separation 63
Chapter 22: Addiction & Substance Use 65

Chapter 23: 67
The Power Of Forgiveness 67
Chapter 24: 69
Practices For Building Force Awareness, Healing, And Bringing Balance To Your Life And The Planet 69
Chapter 25: The Goal Of Emptiness 77
Chapter 26: Plant Medicines & Intoxicant Training 79
Chapter 27: The Lineage Of The Jedi 84
Chapter 28: The Path 86

Dedication

This book is dedicated to my father, Thank you for the undying support, and always believing in me. Also this book is dedicated to my mentor Kevin Marjoram, without who's help, and mentorship I would not have been in a position to write this material.

Acknowledgements

I would like to acknowledge all of my teachers, from the many books on shamanism, and spiritual study, To the courses that I have taken online. A big thank you to the people at Mindvalley, and Jeffrey Allen for sharing the many and various courses on spiritual growth. Thank you to George Lucas for bringing the concept of The Jedi that so many have resonated with on a deeply soul level. Thank you to Alberto Villoldo, who's books, and online courses have helped me grow as a healer. Thank you to my family for all the support throughout my healing journey. Thank you to the readers who have purchased this book, your purchases will help me create an energy medicine school/Jedi temple, and plant medicine retreat center.

About the Author

My name is Jesse Hollis, I am an avid spiritual seeker, as well as a practising energy healer. From an early age I have pursued enlightenment, and the answers to life's mysteries. I travelled to Guatemala at an early age, and visited the ancient city of Tikal, this brought me to an awakening to the world of spirit, and energy, and fuelled my passion for exploring the unknown. At an early age I initiated an atonement process stepping out of coherency, and enlightenment back into the unconscious, this process nearly killed me, and brought about a great deal of suffering. However it also unlocked ancient memory that extends beyond this life into my personal cosmic past. Later I was introduced to a friend, and mentor that is a practising shamanic healer, and this brought me to the fulfillment of my atonement process. Today I am an at home practising energy healer, and author. Pursuing the answers to life's greatest mysteries, seeking healing for myself, and the planet.

You can reach me at jesse.hollis.intirising@outlook.com.

Introduction

Welcome spiritual seekers, This book is intended for those who wish to follow the path to spiritual enlightenment and ascension, with a magical twist on the traditional philosophy. The Jedi Training Manual will teach you what you need to know about the spiritual path to ascension and the light body, and how to live in such a way that your healing spreads to those around you, and to the planet, and beyond.

Drawing from the ancient traditions of meditation and energy medicine this manual provides insight into the deepest mysteries of spiritual progression and enlightenment, while adding the Jedi paradigm to the teachings in a fundamental way in which the reader/student of the manual can envision the bigger cosmic perspective of ascension.

My name is Jesse Hollis, I am energy healer and avid spiritual seeker. My path towards enlightenment started at an early age with the fundamental questioning of all the things I was told while growing up, early contact experiences with extraterrestrials and the paranormal fuelled my questioning. At the age of 18 I travelled to Guatemala and visited the ancient city of Tikal, this visit to an ancient and holy site sparked my awakening, with the experience of being able to feel the energy of the temples. I was not a meditator at the time but still I found myself meditating in the tops of each of the temples, having a clairvoyant vision of the ancient culture that inhabited this site that I would remember years later. I returned home and continued on my path as a youth partying and misusing substances. In 2009

I ingested a substance called 2CI and this opened the doors of perception within my mind, as well as resulted in a psychiatric admission and diagnosis. I moved to Yellowknife, Canada and began my meditation practice and managed to become medication free. My meditation practice led me through an elaborate awakening, this awakening led me to the undertaking of a process of atonement and back into the unconscious. Next years later my father recommended we visit an energy healer he had been recommended to. This re-sparked my interest with meditation and energy medicine, and the healer took me on as an initiate and student. Shortly after resuming my meditation practice I regained an awareness of the atonement process that I had initiated, and began working towards the resolution, and completion of the atonement. Through the atonement I gained many insights into past-life memories and cosmic awareness, a lot of which has contributed to the material I will be sharing in this book.

The reader/student of this manual will be guided through an understanding of The Force, the history of the Jedi on this planet, as well as meditations and techniques for building Force awareness, and even the concepts of plant medicines, and intoxicant training. It is intended for the reader/student of this manual to take only those techniques and philosophies that serve their highest good, and provide the greatest spiritual development possible for the individual. Please do not let these teachings cloud your judgment towards any of the conventional doctrines of medicine or personal development, as all of these philosophies have their place. The reader/student of this manual is expected to take insight within the teachings, and integrate them with conventional philosophy. We may not be completely of this society, but we are within it, take advantage of what serves you within society, and take the teachings that serve your progressive path towards liberation and enlightenment, and leave the rest.

The Jedi Training Manual provides an awareness of both the light and dark sides of The Force, information and knowledge necessary for building One Pointed Force Awareness, and finding oneness and resonance to activate the light body. Included in the manual is a unique vision of a Future Planetary Jedi Order, and concluding in an explanation of the path to come for the reader. Also explanations of meditation, the luminous energy field, and kundalini awakening accompanied by a chapter on the chakras and meridians. We will discuss fear and the shadow, as well as psychic attack and defensive practices. There is a chapter on the medicine wheel, and opening sacred space. There are numerous exercises included in the text to assist the path of learning. I would recommend reading through the entire manual before undertaking the exercises, read the manual in it's entirety, and then go back and follow through with the exercises, and build your daily practice. May this manual assist you in every way possible, The Force is always with you.

Chapter 1: The Jedi

First, we must discuss what it means to be a Jedi. What exactly is a Jedi? What is The Jedi Order? Does it truly exist, and is there any evidence of this?

A Jedi is someone who repeatedly ascends in each incarnation to realize their immortality and has the ability to effect their environment by using telekinetic abilities or someone who is aware of these goals and is actively training to obtain these attributes. A Jedi is much like the shaman or Buddhist monk we find in our society today.

The Jedi Order is the society of these masters that is spread throughout the universe, dedicated to keeping balance throughout the cosmic universe-wide theatrical cosplay of the heroes' journey. These humans are also known as ascended masters.

The Egyptian priests that had telekinetic capabilities were known by the title of "Jedi." All the evidence within the megalithic sites of the planet points towards this planet having been visited in the past by extraterrestrials; it isn't hard to comprehend that a lot of the things we use today and throughout our history including our language, have come from extraterrestrial sources. With that being said, we could make the assumption that the word Jedi meant the same thing throughout the cosmic community as it did to the Egyptian priests and was handed down to the early Egyptians by extraterrestrials, thus handing down to our civilization a lineage of The Jedi.

A Jedi is the master of the elements, bending them at will. This power over the environment The Jedi possess is manipulated not through direct force but rather reciprocity with the environment; the Jedi develops a strong communion with all things. This allows objects to be engaged and moved through thought alone. The person becomes an empty vessel for The Force and can direct it at will. This is demonstrated in spoon bending and other psychic phenomena. When an individual has taken direct action to study these practices, they have become a Jedi initiate. With a lifetime dedicated to this pursuit, mastery can be achieved; it is only a matter of time before we start seeing individuals accomplish these goals and begin ascending beyond the planetary level. Lots of people have been talking about a 5D shift in dimensions taking place on the planetary level. But I prefer to look at us humans as inter-dimensional beings, capable of evolving into inter-planetary beings and achieving God Consciousness, and that there is an awakening taking place within our society on a planetary level, soon we will see these ascensions taking place. Soon, people will begin to harness the inter-dimensional capacities of their bodies, awakening the symbiotic lifeforms within the body that control the light body activation and Force Abilities and connect us with our Jedi lineage.

The Jedi sees beyond the level of the planet, seeing life as an evolutionary path throughout the universe, with the goal being complete cosmic experience and true fulfillment of life's purpose on your chosen path. The Jedi of light ascends with the purpose of peace and balance, keeping order in the universe, and bringing balance to the axis of evil or "service to self" community by opposing them as the hero. While the individuals that choose the dark side follow a path of suffering and glory until they reach a point where they can no longer meet fulfillment in their life due to the karmic entropy that results from defying the foundational oneness of the cosmos, and they then retire back to the side of the light, and benevolence, and continue their journey. There is no right or wrong choice between the light and the dark; everyone has to make that decision for themselves. Both paths are noble, and we will commune in the celebration of all the glorious memories of the concluded heroes' journey on the day that that great time comes. The villains being regarded as heroes in their own right. The path of The Jedi is yours, and the choice is in your hands; the universe awaits, and the lineage of The Jedi is there to support you.

Chapter 2: History Of This Planet

This beautiful planet we call home has a deep and mysterious past. We look back only a few thousand years, and we no longer have much to base anything on other than some artifacts with carbon dating that seem to be in their infancy. Leaving us with not really that much to go from. Then we have all the megalithic sites of the planet that are of great debate as to the ages and creation of such sites.

My insights have led me to a deeper understanding of this planet's past and the lineage of The Jedi. There are many Deities and Gods associated with this planet's past that we find painted and carved into the faces and corridors of these megaliths. Were these extraterrestrials possibly Jedi from elsewhere in the universe that had come here to help initiate civilization on this planet? Does there interaction with us go back to Atlantian times or possibly predate Atlantian times to an era of the past long but forgotten? I would argue that this is the case and that the Jedi Order is responsible for the megaliths and ancient teachings that we see in our world even still today, such as Buddhism and Yoga, that they were responsible for agriculture and technology, and even diplomacy to rise. All of the positive attributes of our society have come from the Jedi.

It is possible that the Jedi have been living on this planet for millions or even billions of years in colonies and even deep within the inner Earth. They may even be living among us throughout our society in the present. There have been many people throughout history who have followed the path of the Jedi and ascension; these people are often responsible for inventions and great feats of innovation or social reform. Many of our great philosophers, scientists, and spiritual masters were and are Jedi on the path of ascension.

Growing numbers of people are in the process of awakening to the awareness of ascension, and immortality. The Jedi visiting us in the past and that are in contact with us today are responsible for this awakening, and they work continuously on the development and arising of this awakening, an awakening to the truth of a Jedi lineage.

Osiris and Quetzalcoatl, and others mentioned throughout this planet's history are examples of Jedi that have interacted with Earth in her past. They brought teachings to the people of the past, such as The Book Of Enoch and the Ten Commandments. Today, the Jedi influence the population with positive messages of awakening and spiritual growth, as well as giving inspiration for new technologies.

My insights tell me that this is a Jedi planet of an ascended master race and that the Jedi from all corners of the universe have been influencing humanity, tracing back to its origins within this cycle of this planet's existence. The body being genetically modified and geared towards ascension and spiritual growth over millions of years, connecting all of us with the cosmic lineage of the Jedi. Over time, this mysterious history will come into a greater perspective, revealing the history of this great Jedi civilization. I believe that this civilization has played the role of being guardians and stewards of the cosmos throughout the cycles of the cosmic past, and that even some of the megalithic sites are remnants of this long-forgotten society, true symbols of the great and mysterious Jedi lineage.

Chapter 3: The Force

The Force, what is the Force? How do we sense it? Is it possible to see it? How do we come into balance with it? How can The Force serve us on our life path?

The Force is all things, the energy between all things, the light and the dark that permeates all things. The Force is Unity, light and dark, an energy field that permeates and spans the entire universe. The Force is balanced, an equal balance of light and dark, positive and negative, masculine and feminine. The Force is Life, The Force is Death. The Force spans all distances of this universe and expands infinitely in all directions beyond. The Force is all-knowing and wise; it is an intelligent energy that informs all things. Nothing can destroy The Force; energy cannot be created or destroyed; the Force has always existed.

The Force flows through our bodies naturally; one must refine the senses in order to perceive this energy flowing. The Force can be used to manipulate the individual's environment. Through developing high reciprocity with all things, the Jedi begins to speak to his environment, developing his/her awareness into Force abilities based on the directed intention on or within the environment. The Jedi intends that the stone float and the visualization of this causes the stone to float; the key is balance and reciprocity with the universe; only when the Jedi can speak in balance to the stone can he lift it.

I have been successfully moving small, light objects using The Force, so I can verify the possibility; telekinesis abilities take a lot of practice to master but get easier with time. However fall away from practice, and the abilities will fade, but they can always be regained through practice.

The Force is studied through the process of meditation and focus practices. Through daily practice of meditation and focus practices, the student achieves one pointed awareness and, through this awareness, begins to perceive The Force and feel its energies. An individual can feel The Force in many ways, such as the wind blowing across the skin.

It is possible to see The Force; you can witness the wind blowing through the trees or blowing the water of the ocean. I also theorize that individuals who require the wearing of glasses are simply witnessing the energy field between objects and clouded energy within the aura, and this phenomenon just needs to be brought into balance, and the vision is repaired at a higher level of sight. This can be done by clearing the cloudy energy within the aura, as this is the distortion we witness; the universe is not out of balance, just the individual is. Through balancing ourselves and clearing distortions within the auric field, we can repair our sight and perceive our surroundings and the energy that connects all things at a higher level.

We come into balance with The Force by immersing ourselves fully in life, paying attention to detail, and observing the world with an open mind. We find balance with the assistance of daily meditation practice, as well as focus techniques that we use on a continual basis. Conscious breathing is a huge asset to coming into balance with The Force and building Force Awareness. Forgiveness creates larger and larger amounts of balance in our lives and allows The Force to flow more freely as we free ourselves from karma. Gratitude for every moment that we live and have lived creates a powerful balance within our lives. Proper rest and diet provide the body with the sustenance that it needs to maintain balance.

The Force serves us on the path of life in many ways; it guides everything we do and gives momentum to all our actions. It allows us to manipulate our environment in ways that serve our purpose. The Force can show us our future, reveal our past, and heal our wounds. There are no limits to what is possible within the capabilities of The Force. Even levitation and flight being available kinetically with these bodies. It is truly amazing all the ways the Force will serve you on this cosmic journey and connect us with the Jedi lineage.

Force Awareness Meditation

Sit comfortably with your legs crossed and your back straight or on a chair or place of your choosing, gently close your eyes, and focus on the breath; allow yourself to become aware of awareness and the consciousness that you are, and let that awareness expand into the space around you, next let that awareness expand further to the area that surrounds your location, letting your awareness surround the earth and expand into interstellar space, let your awareness fill inter-galactic space and encompass the entire universe and then let your awareness expand in all directions, rest in this cosmic state of awareness and allow your feelings to communicate to you, meditate for 5 to 15 minutes in this state, gently open your eyes.

Chapter 4: The Light Side Vs. The Dark Side

Many fear the darkness, fearing the deep, apparent nothingness of the dark. When, in fact, the darkness is just the female energy of the universe and is filled with vibrant energy, it is, in fact, love or the attractive Force, with its opposite being light. Therefore, there is nothing inherently different between these opposing forces of light and darkness other than the masculine and feminine properties. The light being that of the masculine, and the darkness being the feminine energy. Both are equally necessary for all things to exist; it is a balance of the light and the dark that builds everything from the energetic level up.

However, these two polar opposites, within the energetic spectrum, also facilitate and allow for the heroes' journey to exist, with the masculine light providing the sustenance for the hero on his or her journey and the darkness providing the hunger for the villain's rise to power, and conquest. The side of the light seeks to bring the light and dark into balance within themselves, creating peace and harmony that fuels their quest. While the side of the dark seeks to release the light and the obtaining of total darkness to increase their spiritual gravity and gain as much power as possible over their environment.

The side of the light has the advantage of no entropy throughout their quest as the hero, thus creating the conditions for everlasting immortal life to arise outside of being killed along their journey by an adversary. While the side of darkness is in a constant fight with entropy, throughout their progression, gaining ground slowly and reaching a pinnacle that must be reversed in the end, accompanied by all the competitors to the throne of evil that would kill them and claim the throne.

The side of the light will gain more and more density throughout its progression until it reaches an immortal and indestructible state of cosmic existence. While the negative entities must use spooky science, and dark magic to push farther and farther on their conquest, their immortality comes with a cost.

In the end, we all return to the same side of balance, residing in the middle of the two forces, balanced eternally as cosmic friends, no longer adversaries or opponents. This is why forgiveness is so important. You can forgive now or later; forgiveness is the key to ascension, and we all forgive in the end anyway; forgiving now will allow you to progress to mastery, and choosing not to forgive will result in getting stuck within our progression.

So there is the Dark and the Light, both equally important to life throughout the universe; which will you choose? The decision is yours and yours alone, and we will all see each other as friends at the end of this great hero's journey. Power and Glory, or Peace and Love? The lineage of the Jedi is on your side and will guide your quest upon either chosen path.

Chapter 5: Jedi Vs. Sith

As well as the path of The Jedi, there is the opposite path of The Sith; the terms "Jedi" and "Sith" could be compared to the ancient understandings of "Angels" and "Demons." A Jedi is on the path of light and unity and could be referred to as an "Angel," while The Sith are on the path of darkness, separation, and control and could be known as a "Demon." Neither one exists without the opposite, The Jedi playing the part of the hero and The Sith playing the part of the villain. There are many similarities between the paths, but The Sith are fundamentally different in terms of their service to self-progression. The Sith must gain power over their surroundings and enslave as many individuals as possible during their conquest. While The Jedi seeks union with all things, gaining his power through reciprocity and balance. The individual of light will gain awareness of The Jedi of the cosmos and begin receiving their guidance. The person who chooses the path of The Sith and Darkness will begin to receive guidance from the dark intelligence of the service to self-empire. The young Sith will learn to serve their dark master at the top of the empire's power structure and hope to overthrow that master in the future. While The Jedi, on the path of the light, will serve only the greater good of the intergalactic community, and the cosmic lineage of the Jedi.

This evolving world has all the necessities one needs to obtain power on either path, and the body being genetically modified for ascension provides a great start. I am not here to tell you which path to choose; your free will is the most important thing in creation. The hero's journey has a place for all to participate in unique ways. May you find purpose in your chosen path from here into eternity.

Jedi Vs. Sith Meditation: Making The Choice

Sit comfortably with your legs crossed and your back straight or on a chair or place of your choosing, gently close your eyes, and focus on your breath; allow yourself to visualize a path out in front of you; this path is your future as a Jedi or Sith, first allow this future to be filled with all the trials and quests of being a Jedi and obtaining mastery, next let that future dissolve and allow the timeline to be filled with the progression along the path of darkness, seeing yourself conquer and dominate the universe as a Sith Lord, let this visualization fade and simply meditate on the breath for 5 to 15 minutes, gently open the eyes.

Chapter 6: In Order To Find Enlightenment: Chop Wood, Cook Food And Carry Water

The path to enlightenment can be a daunting undertaking. With this in mind, the individual seeking enlightenment will wonder how it is possible to achieve success. There is a Buddhist saying in order to find enlightenment chop wood, cook food and carry water. What this means is that to achieve this great undertaking, one must always take care of the simple things in life. We must take care of ourselves and others. The simple act of doing the dishes or making your bed every morning can bring peace and balance into your life. It is not only meditation and endless spiritual practice that will bring us to the enlightened state; we must take care of the finer points within this life to achieve our goal and obtain liberation. If we neglect our household chores or our personal hygiene, we are neglecting our will to progress and grow. Peace is only possible when your environment reflects that which you seek. Meditation is important, but first, we must chop wood, cook food, and carry water!

Another aspect of chop wood, cook food, and carry water is personal hygiene. As a part of proper personal hygiene, you can consider keeping yourself clean, but you can also consider proper diet, and proper supplementation, as well as regular detox. We will now discuss a healthy diet and proper use of supplements, as well as regular detox.

Healthy Diet & Proper Supplements

The proper use of various supplements accompanied by a healthy plant-based diet will greatly aid you on your path to healing and ascension. There are many ways to approach diet, although I would suggest moving more towards a plant-based diet. The meat that we include in our diet has a very dense energy to it, as it comes from a denser form of life when compared to plants, such as fruits and vegetables. With the adoption of a plant-based or entirely plant-based diet, the individual will not be weighed down by the dense vibration of animal products. Also, you should eliminate processed foods from your diet, as they contain unhealthy fats, and are typically very dense in their nature as well.

Accompanying a healthy plant-based diet, if you can afford supplements, there are a number of these plant-derived compounds that are recommended. Supplements can provide nutrients that we are lacking within our diet, as well as provide powerful detoxifying effects. One issue that many of us suffer from is pineal gland calcification. This can cause many issues and make it harder to connect spiritually. The pineal gland is said to be the "Third Eye," and this all-important gland provides mystical experiences and the ability for inner sight to develop. If this gland has become calcified, its function can be impaired, and the individual may find it harder to connect to the spiritual realms. Below I have listed some beneficial supplements for decalcifying the pineal gland, as well as for detoxing the body, and restoring the brain.

Theracurmin: This supplement contains Turmeric and is a powerful anti-inflammatory and also acts as a detox for the pineal gland.

Fulvic Humic Minerals: This supplement is a powerful detox agent, it removes heavy metals from the body and acts as a powerful detox for the pineal gland.

Cacao: This supplement supports brain health and acts as a detox for the pineal.

Iodine: This supplement is important for overall health and brain function, it also acts as a powerful detox for the pineal gland.

Omega Fatty Acids/DHA: Supplements containing these compounds are great for overall brain health and, in high doses, can fully restore the hippocampus, the center of the brain responsible for memory and internal imaging. It is recommended that a person consume two thousand milligrams of DHA per day to rebuild the hippocampus. This dose is taken before bed for a period of three months for best results, then dropped down in dose for maintenance.

Mimosa Pudica: This supplement is a powerful parasitic detox. Six hundred milligrams to one thousand milligrams should be enough to initiate a fairly powerful response.

Bentonite Clay: This supplement acts as a powerful detox for the colon and will help clear parasites and other toxins while detoxing.

There are countless other supplements that can be taken for various other reasons. I would suggest doing further research regarding supplementation and detox. A proper regimen of those listed above is enough to really assist a plant-based diet and boost health and vitality. In order to gain enlightenment, you must chop wood, cook food and carry water, and all things that support a healthy lifestyle. This will greatly help the progress of the aspiring Jedi.

Chapter 7: The Medicine Wheel & Creating Sacred Space

Before going into the topic of meditation, we will discuss the medicine wheel and the creation of sacred space. It is important in the quest for ascension and immortality to know you are never alone. The medicine wheel and sacred space can help the individual bring in the guiding forces of the earth and cosmos to bring about healing, as well as a sense of companionship. In the tradition I study from the High Andes of Peru, there are specific "Power Animals" that are associated with the four cardinal directions of south, west, north, and east. We find the serpent in the south, the jaguar in the west, the hummingbird in the north, and the eagle or condor in the east. We also have the powerful mother Earth, or "Pachamama," and our star, or "Inti," to call upon. The four directions each have archetypal qualities that comprise them. The south is of the physical and the body. The West is of the mind and emotions. The north is of the ancestors and wholeness, and the east is the domain of spirit. We call upon the power animals of the south, west, north, and east, as well as Pachamama and Inti, our beloved mother earth and father sun, to guide and protect us in our medicine space. Following is an exercise and prayer for opening sacred space.

Opening Sacred Space

Sit comfortably in a place of your choosing, take your hands in prayer position, and then raise both hands together above your head into the eighth chakra that resides a few inches above your head, then opening the eighth chakra to envelop your whole body using your hands by spreading the golden light of the eighth chakra down around your body, next bring your hands back into the prayer position resting in front of you at about chest level and repeat the following.

"To the winds of the south, the great serpent, I call upon you, please bring me healing, help me maintain an awareness of the physical and the body. To the winds of the west, great mother jaguar, guide me on the journey beyond death, teach me to be fearless, guide me to mastery of the mind and emotions. To the winds of the north, great hummingbird, teach me the way of the ancestors, guide me to wholeness, teach me to embark on the great journey into infinity and the world of spirit. To the winds of the east, great eagle/condor, raise me up wing tip to wing tip with the great spirit, teach me the mastery of spirit and the domains of immortality. Pachamama, great mother earth, guide me great mother, help me to ground all the things that no longer serve me, help me to stay grounded deep into the center of the earth. Inti, great father sun, please ground me into the cosmos, illuminate my shadows, please take from me what no longer serves."

Next take your hands from the prayer position and use them to open the sacred space following the prayer, raise your hands straight above your head, and then open the sacred space around you.

Sacred space is an important practice to develop. It provides you with guidance and protection for your medicine work. Always remember to close the sacred space after your meditation or ceremony has concluded. Offer the helping spirits your gratitude, and bid them farewell until your next period of healing work.

Chapter 8: Meditation

The art of meditation is essential to The Jedi's practice. Meditation has its roots deep within the ancient culture of this planet's past; philosophies like Yoga and Buddhism bring teachings and the secrets of the past regarding ascension and light body activation. Other various cultures across the world, such as those of the Americas, have their own philosophies, and the lineage of the Jedi can be found in all the various traditions, as these traditions speak of their connection to "the star brothers."

Meditation will serve you no matter how far your path takes you. We are beings of consciousness, and the act of inward meditation will always serve our progression and purpose. For The Jedi, meditation has a number of uses. The Jedi use meditation for the resting of the body, as well as receiving teachings from guides on a daily basis. Meditation is used for gaining insight into people, places, and objects throughout the life experience of The Jedi, as well as gaining insight into the past and future, as well as the present moment.

Meditation is the act of focusing inward or maintaining a directed focus for a duration of time or indefinitely through life, life is meditation. The Jedi brings a meditative focus to everything he/she does. Meditation drives the progress of The Jedi; with a strong daily practice, you are on your way to mastery. The following is a simple starter meditation.

Beginners Meditation

Sit comfortably with your legs crossed and your back straight or on a chair or place of your choosing, gently close your eyes, next focus on your breath, and simply try to maintain focus on the breath for 5 to 15 minutes, then open your eyes.

Seemingly simple, although it can be difficult at the beginning to maintain focus on the breath. Over time, with practice, you will be able to maintain the focus on the breath for longer and longer, and your practice will be ready to evolve in complexity. In the next chapters, we look at lucid dreaming and then kundalini awakening.

Chapter 9: Lucid Dreaming

Lucid Dreaming is another skill for the developing Jedi. The Jedi initiate will greatly benefit from incorporating the concept of lucid dreaming into their practice. Lucid dreaming means to go from a passive or non-lucid, or even unconscious level of dreaming into a lucid level of dreaming, where the individual becomes aware of the dreaming. In Buddhism, they speak of the waking dream and the dreams of rest and sleep. This means that not only do we dream when we are asleep, but we are also primarily dreaming while we are awake. This concept can be alien to our understanding, but if you simply consider how much of your life is lived from a subconscious awareness, it will become easier to see. We go through most of our waking state in a non-lucid awareness, much the same as our nocturnal dreaming experiences. Through various techniques

that are designed to bridge to unconscious mind with the conscious mind, we gain our lucidity and begin to dream lucidly. The individual who gains lucidity can enter the dreamscape with intention, and even speak to the dream, and interact with the internal dreamer to heal deeply ingrained traumas, and fears.

We will incorporate a few exercises to obtain lucidity and strengthen that lucidity as we move forward. The first is the dream journal that we will bring into our daily practice, journaling our dreams every morning upon awakening. The second is what is called a "Reality Check", where the individual admits to oneself that the nature of the dreams of sleep and the waking dreams that make up most of our experience are very closely related and can be hard to define, especially as you move into lucidity, and the sleeping dreams become even more intertwined, and related to the waking state. A reality check means to accept that you could be dreaming when you think you are awake and perform a specific check to determine whether you are, in fact dreaming and asleep or not. Another technique we can apply to becoming lucid and strengthening that lucidity is called "The Wake Back To Bed Method," this technique is where the individual sets the alarm for after they have been asleep for six or so hours or early in the morning a few hours away from when they will wake in the morning, and allows themselves to wake up temporarily for fifteen minutes, and then goes back to sleep. This allows the mind to come back into waking consciousness and then re-enter the dreamscape with more likelihood of becoming lucid. Finally, we come to the technique of speaking to the dream or speaking with the internal dreamer once lucidity is gained; after awakening within a dream, you simply speak to the dream and ask it to show you something or help you heal something such as fear or trauma, and the dream responds. The following are some exercises you can incorporate into your nightly and daily routine to boost your lucidity and begin living a fully lucid life.

Dream Journal

Every morning, upon awakening, sit down with your journal and ask yourself, "Where was I just before I woke up?", then write down any and all details that come into your awareness. Do this every morning; as you do this exercise, you will be able to recall your dreams better and better, and you will begin to bridge the unconscious mind to the conscious mind.

Reality Check

As you go throughout your day, begin to employ this reality check to begin to bridge the waking and sleep state. Breathe out all the air in your lungs and then pinch your nose shut and with your mouth closed, try to breathe in; if you can breathe in, you are actually asleep and dreaming, and if not, then you are in the waking dimension, next hold your hands out in front of you and twist them while facing you from front to back, do this as fast as you can, twist back and forth then stop with either the front or back of both hands facing you, if you are dreaming your hands will change in form or in some way, if you are awake you will not notice any change. Do this reality check from the time you wake in the morning until the time you go to sleep, whenever you become aware that you might be dreaming, or just when you decide it is a good time to check. Doing this on a daily basis will create a bridge between the waking and sleep states, and soon you will remember to perform the check while you are asleep and dreaming, and you will gain lucidity.

Wake Back To Bed Technique

Now it is time to set your alarm; set it for six hours after falling asleep or for a few hours before you are to awaken in the morning, then upon the alarm sounding in the middle of the night, stay awake for fifteen minutes and then go back to sleep with the intention of becoming lucid. It is not recommended to practice this technique every night, but using it every other day or every third day should be fine; the more you practice this technique, the more you will create a bridge between the waking and sleep state; you can also use the fifteen minutes to write down any dream details in your journal.

Communicating With The Dream

Upon achieving lucidity within a dream, simply call out to the dream to show you something or ask your own internal dreamer to help you heal something. "Dreamer, please help me heal my shadow". The more you gain lucidity and interact with the dream in this conscious way, the more you will dream lucidly and begin to bring lucidity into the waking state.

Lucid dreaming is an extremely powerful and life-transforming practice. By adding these practices to your daily routine, you will strengthen your progress and greatly aid yourself on the path to liberation and ascension as a developing Jedi.

Chapter 10: Kundalini Awakening

Kundalini awakening. Many say there are all sorts of special actions needed to raise the kundalini, but in fact, this sacred energy will rise through simple meditation, with a focus on the breath. The kundalini is the sacred, sexual, and creative energy of the body that has its home in the root chakra at the base of the spine. In meditation, by simply adding an intention to draw the breath up from the root to the top of the head on the in-breath and releasing the kundalini back down the spine on the out-breath, you will begin to awaken this powerful force. Kundalini can result in brilliant visions and various energetic phenomena of the body to arise; simply let them come, let them be, and let them go. With practice, the rising of the kundalini energy will result in samadhi, or a full-body resonance. The following is an exercise to initiate this powerful energy.

Kundalini Meditation

Sit comfortably with your legs crossed and your back straight or on a chair or place of your choosing, gently close your eyes and bring your focus to your breath, long and deep inhales and exhales, focus on staying grounded in the body and deep into the center of the earth, intend on drawing the inhale up from the base of the spine to the top of the head, gently releasing the breath back down the spine, allow any sensations of kundalini to build while maintaining a strong focus on the breath, continue for 5 to 15 minutes, gently open your eyes.

This kundalini meditation will awaken the sacred life force energy within the body and heighten the awareness. Practice this once per day until you begin seeing results. With practice you will be ready to move on with the more complex meditations in the following chapters.

Chapter 11: The Luminous Energy Field

The Luminous energy field is a field of energy that surrounds and permeates the body. This field provides the body with the information it needs to grow and evolve, as well as heal. We must learn to nurture this field of energy by clearing blockages in the chakras and meridians so the luminous energy field is able to properly resonate and sustain itself. Other things, such as diet and exercise, can really help nurture this field as well.

The luminous energy field can be used to travel beyond the body and has several energetic bodies incorporated into its makeup. Twelve of these energy bodies are associated with each of the twelve central chakras, each chakra having a corresponding energy body.

The chakras inform the luminous energy field and provide it with vital energy. The spirit or consciousness that we are attached to the chakra system of the luminous energy field, and through that connection, the luminous energy field manipulates the physical body. In the next chapters, we discuss the Rainbow Body and then the higher self, Followed by a chapter discussing the ego, and then onto The chakras and meridians.

Chapter 12: The Rainbow Body

The Rainbow, or Light Body, is the all-time achievement of the spiritual traditions of this planet. It is essential to The Jedi's progression and ascension. The Jedi ascends as he/she activates their light body and builds in density. The Rainbow Body is discussed in all the various traditions of spirituality found on this planet, commonly referred to as the Christ Body. Today, more and more awareness is building regarding the Rainbow Body and its activation. No longer is this something only monks of the Tibetan monasteries can achieve. By following the exercises outlined in The Jedi Training Manual, the individual will succeed in activating the light body. This will propel the student forward into Force Abilities along the path of ascension and cosmic adventure. The Rainbow body's capabilities are infinite, being capable of flight, levitation, and even teleportation. Giving the individual the required freedom to explore the cosmos. With a strong daily practice, success is in sight. The Jedi Order awaits, and the lineage of the early Egyptian Jedi priests is there to support you on this journey.

Rainbow Body Visualization Exercise

Sit comfortably at a place of your choosing, close your eyes, and focus your awareness on the breath next; visualize your body from the third person, from a place above you, see the body glowing with the radiance of a rainbow, and allow yourself to visualize your rainbow body for 5 to 15 minutes, then gently open your eyes.

This visualization will activate the Rainbow body of the individual and create the conditions necessary to begin strengthening your luminous energy field and achieving resonance.

Chapter 13: The Higher Self

The Jedi initiate finds peace through meditation and spiritual practice. Through dedicated meditation and spiritual practice, the seeker can unlock spiritual guidance, and this guidance can manifest in many ways; it could be a spirit guide that begins communication, answers questions, and guides your path toward ascension. Another form of guidance that can be developed is the connection to the higher self. The higher self is an aspect of the self that could be seen as residing in the future. It is an aspect of the self that knows completely and resides in cosmic awareness. The connection to the higher self resides in the eighth chakra, which sits a few inches above the crown of the head. The individual meditates on the eighth chakra and invites the wisdom and guidance of the higher self into the awareness, and the higher self answers the call. The higher self can teach us many things; it resides in our future in cosmic awareness and thus sees our progression and always knows our best course of action. It supports our quest for immortality and ascension. The higher self also honours the lessons we came into the incarnation with and will maintain the integrity of these lessons above all else. So therefore, we must realize when we ask our questions of the higher self that if we are not receiving an answer, or the answer is not what we expected, we may not be in alignment with our pre-incarnational assignments. The higher self's communication can be received in many ways; it could be a feeling in the body or come through as intuition; it is even possible to hear the voice of the higher self. The following is a meditation practice to build a connection with your higher self.

Higher Self Meditation

Sit comfortably in a place of your choosing, gently close your eyes, and maintain focus on the breath next, bring your hands into prayer position and raise your hands up into the eighth chakra above your head; open the eighth chakra using your hands and envelop the entire body with the golden light of the eighth chakra, next allow your awareness to move from the center of your head up into the eighth chakra, allow your awareness to rest in the eighth chakra, the seat to the higher self, intend or even ask out loud for the higher self to communicate with you, rest in the eighth chakra and be open to any insights or communication, next allow your awareness to descend back to the center of your head and offer a thank you to the higher self, bring your awareness back to your surroundings and gently open your eyes.

Through practising this simple meditation on a regular basis, you will build a relationship with the higher self, and in time the higher self will reach back with guidance. Be patient; it could take time to develop this relationship with yourself.

Chapter 14: The Ego

Now we will go through an analysis of the ego; the ego is a controversial topic, does the ego serve us? Or is it depriving our spiritual progression?

The ego is quite simply our idea of ourselves; it is an elaborate story about our self that has been created throughout our lifetime. This story began within the early years of life, primarily once we experienced our first traumas. The separation that was created in these traumatizing events caused us to begin creating an identity that we felt could not be hurt in the same way as in these early childhood events. The ego was created to protect ourselves, but it was created based on a separation from the external world. Therefore, its illusory nature does not provide an accurate description of the self. This false idea of ourselves propagates the illusory separation and represses our early traumas. The ego hides these events from the self to prevent further injury and protect its creation. Make no mistake: the ego is your creation; it did not come from outside yourself. The ego does not serve our progression spiritually, as it supports the separation that created it. By letting the ego die and realizing the unity of all things, as well as our infinite nature that goes beyond identity, we can heal the separation. This will also allow you to realize your immortality and remember who you truly are, your cosmic identity that goes beyond the incarnational level and stretches into infinity. To progress on the path of the Jedi, one must let their created identity die, and through doing so, the Jedi initiate regains unity and comes to know personal freedom.

Ego Death

Sit comfortably in a place of your choosing, gently close your eyes, and bring your focus to your breath next, bring your awareness to the unity that binds all things and the illusory nature of separation, then allow yourself to see your ego identity, see this story about your self in its entirety, think of your name and all the things you that seem to make you who you are as well as all the things you have been told about who you are, next consciously let go of this story, let it pass from your awareness and let your focus move into infinity, ask yourself "Who am I throughout eternity? What is my cosmic identity?", See your self as an eternal and immortal spirit beyond space and time, connected to all things, say to your self "I am all that is", come back to your breath and bring your awareness back to your surroundings, gently open your eyes.

By practising the ego death exercise, you will set yourself free from the restrictions of separation and limited identity. Step into infinity and your immortal nature; letting the ego die allows the Jedi to embrace the eternal and take a big step towards ascension and immortality.

Chapter 15: Chakras & Meridians

For the purpose of this book, we will now examine the energy centers of the body or "Chakras," as defined by the yogic traditions, as well as an understanding of some of the primary meridians that flow throughout the body. These understandings are fundamental to the practices of this work. There are countless books on the subject of the chakras, and even some that include explanations of the meridians. The explanations found here are sufficient for progress, although I would recommend the reader/student broaden their scope of understanding pertaining to the chakras and meridians. An explanation of the twelve chakras and primary meridians follows.

The 12 Central Chakras

We must now discuss the Chakras or energy centers of the body. There are energy centers spread throughout the entire body, little vortexes of light that maintain balance and are responsible for the manifestation of spirit into the physical. There are twelve central Chakras, seven within the body and five that extend beyond the head, that we will be focusing on. There are countless sub-chakras that make up the energetic network of the body; the pours on our skin are the physical manifestation of these sub-chakras. With an understanding of the chakras and how they operate, the individual can use the power of the chakras to fuel their manifestations and spiritual growth. The chakras are little vibrant vortexes of light that spin clockwise or counter-clockwise, depending on the individual.

Clearing the energetic sludge that accumulates in these energy centers throughout life is an important practice; chakra-clearing exercises are found at the conclusion of this chapter.

With beautiful, bright, glowing chakras that are clear of stagnant energies, the individual has an increased manifestation ability and has become a clear channel for The Force to flow through. Over time, the individual gains a sensitivity towards feeling these energy centers and can clear them in a moment's time. The following is an explanation of the twelve chakras that we will focus on here in this work.

Root Chakra: The root chakra is located at the base of the spine and points down to the ground as well as forwards and backwards. It is the chakra of awareness, the sexual center of the body. It is also the chakra that grounds all we manifest into the physical. This chakra refines our manifestations and makes them practical for creation. This chakra promotes an awareness of the physical balance and the healing systems of the body. Activation of the first chakra results in freeing the kundalini, unlocking this sacred energy at the base of the spine to flow freely. This chakra grounds us to the planet that we find ourselves on at any given time throughout our cosmic journey and grounds us into reality in the depths of space. This chakra is red in colour.

Second Chakra: The second chakra, or "Hara," is located just below the navel, pointing forwards and backwards from the body. This chakra is responsible for self-awareness. It allows the individual the sense of I am. It is the emotional center of the body, the furnace that burns off toxic energies. This energy center fuels our manifestations with all the energy they require. This chakra is connected to the hand chakras, and the second chakra sends energy to the hands like a fuel tank for the hand chakras to do healing work. When activated this chakra allows the individual an awareness of the emotional body. This chakra is orange in colour.

Solar Plexus Chakra: The solar plexus chakra is located at the solar plexus just below the center of the chest, pointing forward and backward from the body. This chakra is the powerhouse of the body, fuelling the body with its vital energies. This chakra is the chakra of self-identity, as well as the choice between the positive and negative polarities. This chakra adds momentum to our manifestations; it generates power within the manifestation you are working with. With the activation of the third chakra, we come to the place of "the integrated self". This chakra is yellow in colour.

Heart Chakra: The heart chakra is located at the center of the chest, pointing forward and backward from the body. This chakra is responsible for authentic feelings, compassion, gratitude, forgiveness, grace, humility, joy and bliss. This chakra is responsible for unity consciousness; it is the chakra that causes us to look to the stars and know we are not alone. This chakra purifies our manifestation; it ensures we are acting selflessly in the manifestation process. This empowers our manifestations and enriches our experience of obtaining our goals. This chakra is the central chakra of the body, providing all the necessary balance required through life. With the activation of the heart center, we gain "Cosmic Awareness." This chakra is green in colour.

Throat Chakra: The throat chakra is located at the neck and points forward and backward from the body. This chakra is responsible for communication and insight as it is the center of love and light, the center of wisdom. It provides the individual with the motivating energies necessary for psychic abilities. As the fourth chakra is the chakra of balance, the fifth is the chakra that allows you to understand this balance. This chakra allows us to communicate our manifestations to the universe. This is the chakra of telepathy. With the activation of the fifth chakra, the individual awakens their telepathic abilities and obtains deep inner wisdom. This chakra appears blue in colour.

Third Eye Chakra: The third eye chakra is located behind the brow on the forehead in the center of the head and points forward and backward from the body. This chakra is the seat of the soul, the psychic center of the body. It is the chakra that we add all the creative spark to our manifestations; it is where we design the manifestations from. This is the center of unity and love. This center is the gateway to intelligent infinity and cosmic wisdom. This center is responsible for psychic vision or clairvoyance, as well as clairaudience, which is the ability to hear guidance. This chakra is the center of energetic awareness. With the activation of the sixth chakra, the individual activates all of their psychic potential. This chakra is indigo colour.

Crown Chakra: The crown chakra is located at the top of the head. This chakra is the center of cosmic awareness and God Consciousness. It is where we hold our concepts of intelligent infinity. It is the center responsible for our comprehension of the infinite. This chakra is the vortex in the body that draws the energies of the soul down into the body. This chakra allows the individual to have an experience of god and oneness. Activating this energy center allows the individual to understand the cosmos. This chakra is violet in colour.

Eighth Chakra: The eighth chakra is located above the head by a few inches. This chakra is responsible for immortality and awareness that extends beyond incarnations. The eighth chakra acts as the vehicle between incarnations; all of the other chakras upload into the eighth upon death, and we begin our life review and preparations for our next incarnation. The eighth chakra is the seat to the higher self and is the chakra that connects us with our higher self. Upon activation of this chakra, we gain insight into past lives and awareness beyond the present incarnation. The eighth chakra is golden in colour, appearing like a golden sun.

Ninth Chakra: The ninth chakra is located a few inches above the eighth and is the chakra of spirit. It is the chakra of inter-dimensionality and transmutation. This chakra connects us to the spirit realms and the underworld as well as the bardo realms. This chakra connects us to the dreamscape and is where the dreamer resides. Activating this chakra allows for lucid dreaming and inter-dimensional travel, such as the shamanic journey. This chakra manifests as a brilliant white light.

Tenth Chakra: The tenth chakra is located a few inches above the ninth. It is the chakra of transcendence. It allows us to go beyond our regular capacities into the supernatural levels that transcend our natural levels of God's Consciousness. It is the springboard chakra of the upper celestial chakras. This chakra carries the capacity for resurrection. Activating this chakra allows one to transcend death. This chakra is turquoise green in colour.

Eleventh Chakra: The eleventh chakra is located a few inches above the tenth. It is responsible for spiritual growth as it pulls from the top of the system all the way from the root and feeds the twelfth chakra with all the energies needed to produce ascension. Activating this chakra allows one to step boldly onto the path of immortality. This chakra is cobalt orange in colour.

Twelfth Chakra: The twelfth chakra is located a few inches above the eleventh. This chakra is responsible for ascension and the full realization of immortality. With the activation of all the central chakras from the root up to the twelfth, the individual activates their immortal body. With the acceptance of immortality as something that is natural, the twelfth chakra activates and propels the individual into eternity. This chakra is a vibrant neon rainbow merkaba.

The Major Meridians

There are several meridians that we will focus on in this book. These meridians are key to the meditations outlined in the material. There are the two meridians of the legs, both running up the legs from the feet into the root chakra at the base of the spine. A single meridian runs from the base of the spine to the top of the head, following a central alignment much in line with the spine. Two meridians that run down the back perpendicular to the central meridian, and two that run up the front of the body perpendicular to that central meridian. Accompanied by one meridian running down each shoulder into each arm and out each hand, connecting the arms into the other meridians.

There are countless other meridians that connect all the primary chakras, as well as all the sub-chakras throughout the body. They are responsible for sending energy to the various areas of the body, supplying the glands and organs with their fuel for operation. With an understanding of the primary meridians, the reader/student becomes aware of the energetic flows throughout the body and begins clearing blockages throughout this system; doing so, the student achieves balance and homeostasis, bringing their body into an increased state of healing and repairing the luminous energy field. Clearing these channels allows The Force to flow freely and unobstructed throughout the body.

The primary chakras and meridians are essential to the practice, giving the student a greater sense of the energies of the body. Over time this awareness extends to the various sub-chakras and tertiary meridians, allowing the student to fine-tune their system and keep a strong momentum towards their progression. Next, we will include a couple of chakra and meridian clearing exercises.

Chakra Clearing Exercise

Sit comfortably with your legs crossed and your back straight or on a chair or place of your choosing, close your eyes and allow yourself to focus gently on the breath, visualize the twelve central chakras within the mind's eye, start at the root chakra and take one of your hands and spin the chakra in the opposite direction to its natural spin thus putting the chakra into a backwash, using your intuition to determine the direction of spin, gently use your hand to grab onto any stuck energies that reside in the chakra, next take energy with your hand from the beautiful glowing eighth chakra and fill the chakra that has just been cleared with this golden light, now spin the chakra back into its natural direction, move on to clear all of the central chakras following this process.

Clearing Your Chakras In The Shower

Start your shower, and when you are ready to step inside, begin by spinning all seven of the central chakras within the body from the root to the crown in their opposite direction and this will put your energy system into a backwash and cleansing cycle and allow the water of the shower to wash the sludge and stuck energies from the chakras, use your hands to pull and energies that do not free easily, finish by filling the chakras with energy from the eighth chakra and spinning the chakras back to their normal direction, use your intuition to discern the directional spin of your chakras.

Visualization For Clearing The Primary Meridians

With your eyes open or closed in any setting, allow yourself to focus on the breath next visualize energy flowing into the feet and up the legs into the root chakra and overflowing into your grounding cord and deep into the earth, then visualize energy entering and activating the crown chakra, let this energy flow down the back two meridians that are perpendicular to the central meridian down into the root chakra, now bring that energy up the front two meridians and allow this energy to flow out the crown and down the aura in all directions and down into your grounding, at your neck let the energies split and travel down each arm and out the hands, allow this flow to accompany the breath, visualize any blockages that you feel entering this flow and exiting through your grounding and into the earth.

With the understanding of the chakras and meridians, accompanied by these exercises to clear them, the individual is equipped with all he/she needs to progress on the path of The Jedi. Clearing the energy centers and meridians to provide balance and flow within the necessary systems. The reader/student gains healing and insight through the clearing process, becoming a clear channel for The Force and joining with the lineage of Jedi who have come before.

Chapter 16: Gaining Focus And Building One Pointed Force Awareness

Gaining focus, and building your One Pointed Force Awareness. In order to gain focus, you must first start by introducing a meditation practice to your daily routine. There are a handful of other techniques that will be useful to building your focus, and gaining One Pointedness. Strong meditation practice is the single most important thing for gaining one-pointedness; as we meditate, our energies consolidate and come into coherency, and we coalesce on the focal point within. This greatly enhances our focus while adding an open-eye meditation incorporating a fixed gaze on an object across from you for prolonged periods of time. These practices will help you find One Pointedness and a greater focus.

As your awareness increases, you will become more and more aware of your surroundings. Conscious breathwork, and maintaining a strong focus on the breath all the way through your day will lead to greater levels of focus, and all of these practices will open the gateway of One Pointed Force Awareness. With this awareness will come a coherent perception of the flowing energy in the body and an energetic resonance of the whole body that will last beyond meditation into the rest of your day. Awareness will expand to your surroundings in an energetic way over time with practice. The following is a starting point for a daily practice to begin building Force Awareness.

Focus Meditation

Sit comfortably with your legs crossed and back straight or in a chair or place of your choosing, close your eyes, relax your entire body, and allow all your energy to return from all places, people, and things. Focus on grounding yourself into your body and deep into the center of the earth; next, just meditate for 5 to 15 minutes on where you really are, and maintain a strong focus on the breath... you are within yourself, but take some time to sit and recognize this place, your true home, and gently open your eyes.

Open Eye Meditation

Sit comfortably with your legs crossed and back straight or in a chair or place of your choosing and have an object across from you at about eye level; anything will do; you could even put a dot on a piece of paper with a circle around the dot and use the dot for focusing on, next, relax your body and allow all energies to return to you from places, people and things, focus on grounding yourself into your body and deep into the center of the earth, focus on your breathing and maintain a focus on the object for 5 to15 minutes.

Sleep/Rest Meditation

Lie down on your back comfortably on your bed or where you intend on sleeping, close your eyes, relax your entire body, beginning at your head and moving down to your feet, maintain a strong focus on your breath, and just relax and let go of the day you have just retired from, let go of all your concerns and daily stresses and just relax, focus on your breathing, long and deep breaths, maintain this meditation for 5 to 15 minutes or until you fall asleep or continue meditating through your night replacing sleep with conscious rest or until you become too tired and simply roll over and sleep.

These three initial practice meditations are great for creating your initial daily practice, and the first two meditations can be increased in duration as you become more and more comfortable with the practice. The Sleep/Rest meditation is optional at the start; you will want to add it to your day for the best results, and it is flexible and can be mastered to varying degrees; a lot of healing will come from replacing sleep with conscious meditation, although it will take some work, with practice it can be achieved and when we do, we step into the totality of planetary, and cosmic consciousness, moving beyond the one revolution of the planet, and into our immortality. Remember that this is a goal we keep throughout our lifetime. It will take time to master.

Chapter 17: Oneness, Samadhi And Resonance: Light Body Activation

The Jedi's progression relies on gaining a state of oneness. Through the gaining of oneness within your daily meditation practice, you will begin to reach a vibrational resonance or samadhi, which is, in fact, the activation of the light body.

Breathwork, as well as a yoga or qigong workout, will help your body's energies come into alignment and strengthen this process. You can add this in when you are ready; there are a number of books and online courses on yoga and qigong; find something that works for you and build a physical meditation into your daily practice; a strong physical fitness routine can also be a powerful physical meditation practice.

When you begin achieving a resonance that sustains itself, you have moved forward in the process from activating the light body to strengthening it. The process of entering and re-entering samadhi, or resonance, will build your energetic density over time, making it easier for you to sense The Force in all of its manifestations and begin affecting your surroundings. As we continually re-enter samadhi, we will be confronted by our wounds, both of this life and of previous incarnations. Do not ignore these painful feelings as they arise; allow yourself to feel compassion for yourself and these feelings associated with the trauma. Over time, these feelings will subside as they are healed with each encounter of the oneness.

The levels of samadhi are infinite; you will continue to reach higher and higher levels of resonance. Stay focused on grounding yourself into your body and deep into the center of the earth. As you do this, you will begin to perceive the energetic flows of the body. In later chapters, we will learn to direct these flows into a positive loop that will keep us grounded in the body and centered in the healing state. Contrary to what most may think, healing and spiritual progress doesn't come from leaving the body; we progress spiritually by integrating our consciousness deeper and deeper into the body; this is the art of ascension.

Over time, as you will gain confidence in your ability to enter samadhi, you will begin to have great insight into these states of resonance. These insights will unlock the understanding necessary for Force Awareness and Force Capabilities. Stay diligent with your practice, and devote as much time as you can spare to honing your abilities.

Oneness Breathwork Meditation

Sit comfortably with your legs crossed and back straight or on a chair or place of your choosing, close your eyes, relax the entire body and allow all energies from places, people and things to return, Allow the mind to relax and begin to focus on the breath, long and deep inhales and long drawn out exhales, in through the nose and out through the mouth and focusing on your grounding, do this for several minutes and allow yourself to find a flow with the breath, next breathe in and out through the mouth, do this with a higher intensity of forcefully breathing all the way in and then all the way out, build some momentum with the in and out breath and then when your are ready, all the way out and all the way back in and hold at the top of the breath, hold as the vibrational resonance builds and then release the breath out through the mouth followed by a slow in breath through the nose and then return to the long, deep relaxed breath, then repeat this 5 to 10 times, at the end of the repetitions relax and breathe calmly and reflect in silent meditation for several minutes, gently open your eyes.

This meditation can be increased in duration by increasing the number of repetitions done and increasing the sitting time afterwards. Feel free to incorporate other breathwork techniques into this meditation. There are countless ways to enter resonance or samadhi, this is just one way I have found works for anyone. If you have a practice routine that leads you to a state of resonance already, that is great, and keep using it.

Eventually, breathwork becomes unnecessary to reach samadhi, and it becomes effortless as we focus on relaxed breathing. The kundalini rises, and energetic resonance builds. This practice of achieving resonance will carry you on the path of the Jedi to the halls of immortality, continually strengthening the light body and increasing the body's longevity. Oneness is key.

Chapter 18: The Future Planetary Jedi Order

With the current state of affairs throughout the society we see today, it's hard to know what the future will bring. My vision of the future is that, at some point, the awakening will reach a critical mass and envelop the planet. We will see a shift away from technology towards the domains of spirit and energy. Our people will seek the truth of who we are as a species and seek to know our brothers and sisters from the stars. We will generate a new education system, teaching Force Awareness and Force Abilities, as well as Force Healing, that will replace the current education and medical systems. We will move away from our ideas of separation and into a state of civilizational Unity.

This will propel us into an interplanetary civilization, seeking the answers to the universe's greatest mysteries. We will grow to be guardians and teachers within the cosmic community. Joining our star brothers in eternity. Joining with the Jedi Order that spans the universe, learning from the ascended masters that preceded us, and merging with the great lineage of Jedi who have come before us.

We will build Jedi training temples and grand archives of the universe's history and all its inhabitants. We will bring balance to the cosmos once again.

Future Vision Meditation

Sit comfortably with your legs crossed and your back straight or on a chair or place of your choosing, close your eyes, relax your body, and allow all energies to return from places, people, and things; focus on grounding yourself into your body and deep into the center of the earth, maintain awareness of the breath and allow your awareness to rest in the future, simply project your awareness onto the generalized idea of the future, next allow that future to become filled with all the progress from the present leading to that future Jedi civilization, allow your mind to fill in the details and when the process gets stuck simply improvise some details that keep the process filling in, allow yourself to feel gratitude for this future and what you are able to perceive. Allow this meditation to find a duration that works for you and still allows for immersion in this future vision. Return to the present and your surroundings, and gently open your eyes.

Chapter 19: Fear & The Shadow

Fear is the path to the dark side; the Jedi must face the darkness within to progress on the path of light and ascension. Many talk about fear; there are many philosophies regarding this all-important topic. It is crucial to realize that fear is an illusion, an illusion cast by the inner shadow of the subconscious mind. The shadow is seen in many ways, but it is simply the aspects of oneself that are hidden deep within the subconscious. Early trauma in one's experience causes a separation in the mind, creating compartmentalization within the mind. One of these compartments is seen as the shadow.

The Jedi must face these hidden aspects of the mind and heal the trauma of the past. By doing so, the Jedi student unlocks deeper healing and ascension experiences. The shadow stands between the student and cosmic awareness; much various awareness, such as past life recall, become known as one that heals the shadow and inner traumas. At the root of all fear is the fear of death and the fear of the creator or universe. The individual fears death and the uncertainty of the final experience of an incarnation, accompanied by a fear that the universe or creator will hold us accountable for all the things we view ourselves punishable for. By seeing through this illusion and recognizing universal love and unity, the seeker is liberated from fear and can then unlock deep healing and ascension towards immortality.

Through forgiveness and reason, the Jedi finds atonement and equanimity, moving beyond the confines of fear and inner darkness towards the path of infinity. The simple realization that the creator or universe knows only love and unity liberates one from the snares of fear and shadow; through this realization, we see that the universe is a place of infinite life and infinite love, and therefore, our fears are total illusion and nothing else.

Recognition of Fear and Healing the Shadow

Sit comfortably in a place of your choosing and gently close your eyes, maintain awareness of the breath and allow yourself to become centered and focused, next allow your awareness to include your fears, allow yourself to contemplate death, visualize your eventual passing from this incarnation, visualize the life planning stages between incarnations and the eventual reincarnation into a new body, next allow yourself to feel forgiveness, for yourself and for anyone who has brought you pain, say to yourself "I forgive myself, I forgive everyone" and ask yourself "does the universe hold me or anyone accountable for our actions and deal out punishment as a result of our actions?" allow yourself to feel unity, project your awareness from your body out into the surrounding area and allow this to expand into space and to keep expanding into inter-galactic space and beyond into infinity, ask yourself "does a universe of unity allow for judgment?", next allow your awareness to return to your body and come back to your surroundings, gently open your eyes.

By practising this simple visualization on a regular basis, the student is capable of releasing internal fears and begins to heal the shadow. Moving forward, we will discuss psychic attacks & defensive practices.

Chapter 20: Psychic Attack & Defensive Practices

As a developing Jedi, the student must realize that upon the path of light and ascension, we will encounter darkness and the forces that oppose us. This brings us to the subject of psychic attacks and defensive practices. Psychic attack can manifest in numerous ways and will be unique to the individual experiencing it. Even though the ways that a psychic attack can manifest are various, there are some basic visualization and meditation techniques that can be followed to prevent a psychic attack or put an end to an attack that is being experienced. In some cases, the attack may be so severe that these techniques may seem to have no effect on the attack; maintain your diligent daily practice, and remember that within a severe psychic attack, the strongest defence can be to persevere through the attack with love in your heart, and a strong focus on the light within all things. The smallest hint of light can be a powerful defence against the powers of darkness. Continue to heal your personal shadow and trauma, as the affinity for the attack lies within these weak links within the mind.

The sources of psychic attack are various, It can be that it comes from someone of this world, or it can originate from beyond this world; as we progress on our path of ascension, we draw attention to ourselves from beings that are beyond this planet and would seek to bring an end to our progression. When being faced with a psychic attack, we must remember that although an attack may come from a peer within this world, it is unlikely that our negative peers throughout society have the power necessary to produce a substantial attack. Most psychic attack comes from entities that dwell beyond the planet, even within cases where one of our peers of this world is casting an attack upon us; they are usually calling upon forces greater than themselves to accomplish the attack. This is an important detail; when we are dealing with a psychic attack, we are usually dealing with an entity that dwells beyond this planet and is of an advanced level of consciousness. This may seem like a hopeless encounter, but always remember that the reason why the attack was initiated by an entity of a highly developed nature is because they fear your progress within the path of ascension; you are a threat to their dark agenda upon this planet. I myself have been faced with a severe psychic attack for more than a decade. I always remember that the reason why I go through this painful experience is because of my progress towards ascension and the fear this brings to the powers of darkness. The following are a couple of techniques that can help prevent an attack or bring an end to the attack already being experienced.

Aura Cleansing and Reinforcement

Sit comfortably in a place of your choosing, allow your eyes to gently close and maintain a focus upon your breath, visualize golden light coming down from above the higher chakras above the head and entering your auric field; visualize this golden light cleansing your aura, allow the golden light to burn up the impurities and heavy energies within the aura, next visualize these toxic energies leaving the aura down into the earth, call upon the spirit of mother earth to help, now continue to visualize the golden light entering the aura, allow this energy to fill the aura and gain in density, continue filling the aura for as long as you feel necessary, once you feel you have sufficiently strengthened the aura gently open your eyes.

Aura Cleansing and Banishing Ritual Using Incense

Stand comfortably in a place of your choosing, take the incense of your choosing, and light the purifying substance using your match or lighter once burning while holding the incense within your hand, spin counterclockwise in a circle, slowly and deliberately drawing a sacred circle around yourself, next spin clockwise drawing a sacred circle in the other direction while keeping an intention that you are the only one allowed within this space, next standing within the sacred circle take the incense and pass it throughout your entire auric field bringing purity to the auric field. Call upon the guardians or arch angels to protect your sacred space, call upon the lineage of the Jedi for guidance and protection, and remember that this space belongs to you and you alone; keep your space for yourself, and give the rest of the universe over to everyone else. Put out the incense safely.

By following these two exercises, you will strengthen the auric field and protect against psychic attack. Always remember if this does not seem to work, perseverance and focus upon the love and light within all things is your best defence. Along with your daily practice, including the other practices found within this manual, you will strengthen yourself and your energy system, and no matter how severe an attack may be, you will find liberation.

Chapter 21: Trauma & Separation

Now we will discuss trauma and the separation that is created through this trauma. Trauma is an injury that can be physical, as well as psychological, or even spiritual. Trauma is stored within the body and mind. This trauma creates a separation within the mind; early childhood events that cause trauma cause the individual to turn away from connectedness and unity and to create a separation between themself, and the external world. This separation causes stress on the individual as they move away from unity. The trauma is then compartmentalized within the mind and stored physically in the tissue of the body. The trauma is then repressed and forgotten. This results in stress on the body and mind and creates disease. Through spiritual practice and mindfulness, the individual can heal these traumas and heal the separation. By seeing the unity of all things and seeing that separation is an illusion, the trauma is healed. It is possible through the practice of recapitulation to uncover these repressed and hidden traumas. The following is an exercise to help you identify the hidden trauma and begin to heal the separation.

Recapitulation And Trauma Identification

Sit comfortably in a place of your choosing, gently close your eyes and bring your focus to your breath, next allow yourself to move into the past with your awareness, moving from the present back to the previous day and then from there to a few days previous, move further to a week ago and then a month ago, next to six months ago and then to a year in the past, keep moving into the past using any of the highlights of your life that you remember, two years, three years and then to five and ten years, follow this process until you arrive in your early childhood going back as far as you can, if you notice any traumatic events or memories simple let them enter the mind and let them be without judgment and then let them go and continue to move into the past, once you have successfully recapitulated your entire life simply focus on the breath and let it all go bringing your awareness to the unity of all things, allow yourself to see that separation is an illusion for all is connected through energy, then when you are ready bring your awareness back to your surroundings and gently open your eyes.

Practising this process of recapitulation will allow you to uncover hidden aspects of your past, remember traumatic events, and begin to heal them. Just remember, as the difficult memories begin to come back, simply let them come, let them be, and let them go. In the next chapters, we will talk about addiction and substance use, and then the power of forgiveness, then onto some practices for building force awareness and healing ourselves and the planet.

Chapter 22: Addiction & Substance Use

Something that can stand in the way of the developing Jedi is addiction and substance use. Along the path of life, we encounter trauma, as talked about previously. This trauma lives in the unconscious mind and can manifest as an addiction to various substances. The unhealed wounds of our past cause us pain, and it is often a pain that we don't understand. Quite often, people with unhealed trauma reach to substances to mask or cover up this pain. Although we find relief in these destructive habits, they will limit our progression upon the path of ascension. The Jedi student should seek to be free of all attachments and, therefore, should also seek freedom from addictions. This could be as simple as a dependency on coffee to wake yourself every morning, or it could be as serious as a cocaine addiction. Understand I am not condemning anyone for substance use; I myself suffered with a cocaine addiction for close to a decade. The important thing is there is always hope, and you can free yourself from these destructive habits.

When facing an addiction, it is important to have faith and find faith in a power greater than yourself. This could be god or The Force, or any number of things; the important thing is to have a source of a higher power that you can look to for guidance and inspiration. The aspiring Jedi can call upon the universe and call upon The Force for this support and healing. It is also important to have someone to talk to about your situation, a friend or family member that can listen and support you on the path to sobriety.

The important thing to realize when facing an addiction is that you are covering up the pain of long-repressed trauma. Begin looking at the nature of the pain and begin asking the hard questions about the pain's origins. Realize that substance use is not going to heal the pain, and your healing depends upon sobriety.

It is important for the developing Jedi to maintain a sober and balanced lifestyle. Begin to liberate yourself from any and all destructive habits and free yourself from all addictions. Always remember you are not alone, and nothing is ever hopeless.

Chapter 23: The Power Of Forgiveness

The power of forgiveness is essential to the path of the Jedi. Along the path of ascension, there will be many challenges; some of these trials may be quite painful. Therefore there will be the necessity for forgiveness to heal these traumas. Forgiveness has the power to heal trauma and fear; forgiveness is the path towards love and unity. Through forgiving all the people who have hurt us along our progression, we liberate our emotions and heal our minds. The Jedi of Light will need to forgive all those who have caused pain, as well as forgiveness of the self, in order to progress farther along the path towards enlightenment. The hero's journey is a journey of the light as well as the dark. Therefore, there will always be pain and conflict. When facing these trials, the Jedi initiate uses forgiveness to abolish the darkness and embrace love, and unity. Through the power of forgiveness, the Jedi atones for all the karmic ties that keep the student bound to the past and tied to the wheel of karma and incarnation. Forgiveness allows individuals to liberate themselves from the cycles of reincarnation, birth, and death. Moving forward into eternity and immortality. At the conclusion of the grand heroes' journey, all participants will be seen as equal no matter who they have wronged or however much pain they have caused; therefore, there is no real answer but to forgive and free yourself from karma. The following is an exercise in forgiveness.

Forgiveness Exercises

Sit comfortably in a place of your choosing, gently close your eyes and maintain focus on the breath; allow yourself to visualize all the people in your past that have hurt you or caused you pain, and allow the images of their faces to fill your mind, allow any details about the trauma to surface and fill the inner landscape, next say out loud or internally "I forgive you, and I forgive myself," allow all of the images and stories of the past pass from your mind, gently open your eyes.

Through practising regular forgiveness in your meditation practice, as well as throughout your daily life, you will set yourself free. Begin on your healing journey!

Chapter 24: Practices For Building Force Awareness, Healing, And Bringing Balance To Your Life And The Planet

Next, the Jedi initiate must broaden his/her meditation practice by adding a few other techniques into their daily meditation and practice. In this section, we will be combining all three meditations, the Open Eye Mediation and the Oneness Breathwork Meditation, as well as a visualization of the Future Jedi Order and your place within it. We will also include a visualization to set up a positive loop within the body that will accompany the focus on the breath and will keep you grounded in the body. The student will use the understanding of the chakras and meridians to achieve this.

Positive Energy Loop Visualization

In this visualization, we will be using various meridians throughout the body that you are aware of from the previous chapter on the chakras and meridians. There are two meridians that run down the back of the individual and runs perpendicular to the central channel from the top of the head to the base of the spine into the root chakra. Then, there are two meridians that run up the front of the body opposite to the ones on the back. We will also be visualizing the meridians of the legs.

Positive Energy Loop Visualization

Visualize energy entering your feet and travelling up your legs and into the root chakra, where the energy overflows and travels down your grounding cord at the base of the spine down into the center of the earth. Allow this flow of energy to accompany the breath; next, visualize energy entering your crown chakra and activating the crown; allow that energy to split into the two rear meridians and travel down to the root chakra. Next, direct that energy back up the front two meridians and out the crown chakra, showering out in all directions and down your aura into the grounding. Also, allow this energy to split at the neck and travel down each arm and out the hands; allow the flow in the legs and upper body to naturally flow with the breath.

This visualization is very powerful and can be taken into the rest of your day; as you maintain focus on the breath throughout the day, simply focus part of your intention on running your energy through this flow system. Over time, your sensitivity to feel these currents circulate will increase. This visualization will clear energy blockages, strengthen the energetic system of the body, and promote healing. Next, we will combine the three meditations into one.

Advanced Force Awareness Meditation

Sit comfortably with your legs crossed and your back straight, close your eyes, relax the entire body starting at the head and moving down to the feet, let go of any tension and stress, let go of worries about health and dying, letting go of all attachments and negative thoughts, let go of blame and judgment, allow all energies to return from places, people and things, focus your attention on the breath and ground yourself into your body and the earth, next visualize energy entering your feet and travelling up your legs and into the root chakra where the energy overflows and travels down your grounding cord at the base of the spine down into the center of the earth, allow this flow of energy to accompany the breath, next visualize energy entering your crown chakra and activating the crown, allow that energy to split into the two rear meridians and travel down to the root chakra, next direct that energy back up the front two meridians and out the crown chakra showering out in all directions and down your aura into your grounding, also allow this energy to split at the neck and travel down each arm and out the hands, allow the flow in the legs and upper body to naturally flow with the breath, relax into the visualization and long deep breathes, continue in stillness and silence for 10 to 15 minutes or a time that is comfortable, then begin the deep forceful breathing in and out of the mouth and holding at the top of the breath and sustaining resonance, repeat this 10 to 15 times then allow the breath to return to normal and then back to a long and deep breath in and out, allow yourself to sit in stillness for 10 to 15 minutes or as long as comfortable, then opening the eyes and fix the gaze on the object across from you and maintain the positive energy loop visualization, continue gazing at the object for 10 to 15 minutes then close the eyes and visualize yourself sending positive energy to all things of the universe for several minutes in gratitude for all that exists, next visualize the future Jedi Order as described before and this time allow yourself to become a part of that vision, visualize yourself as a Jedi master in that future with all the Force abilities you can think of accompanied by your contributions to the evolving Jedi civilization, letting yourself relax and let go of the visualizations and just breathe and relax for several minutes. Come back to your surroundings and gently open your eyes.

Bring this meditation into your daily practice at least once per day; the more frequently you practice, the stronger your Force Awareness will become. Gaining powerful insight and strength of resonance will follow.

Levitating An Object

Next, you will add another exercise to your routine. From now on, you will take 5 minutes a day to practice levitating an object; I would recommend something small and lightweight as you can more easily shift the balance on the palm of your hand; there are countless objects that can be incorporated into this exercise, choose one that works for you. But be creative and find some small object that you can place on one of your palms and use the other hand to shift the balance or move the object with the ultimate goal of levitating the object using the energy of the opposite hand. The key is realizing that the universe is alive, even the objects that we consider inanimate. You must speak to the object with your mind as you reach with the energy of the other hand and visualize the object beginning to float. The more you exercise this practice, the more you will condition your mind to know the possibility, and you will eventually succeed.

With this as a daily practice, you will succeed on the path of the Jedi and ascension, as the practical levitation exercise brings the practice into the realm of physical manifestation through the interactions of the energetic world, making your progress a tangible and physical experience.

Conscious Meditation Replacing Sleep

Next, we will discuss conscious meditation replacing sleep. As your meditation abilities grow, the duration of the night you can consciously meditate will increase, with the goal being that of completely replacing sleep with conscious meditation. This will be difficult at the beginning, but with practice, you will reach farther and farther towards the sunrise of the next day. At first, you will make it only so far, but as you train your body to enter deeper brainwave states like theta and gamma, you will eventually sustain meditation through the entire night. By adding the positive energy loop visualization to your nightly practice, you will engage the body's healing system directly, and your progression will exponentially increase. Take this meditation template into your nightly conscious rest practice.

Conscious Rest Meditation

Lie down on your back in your bed or where you intend on resting for the night, relax your entire body with your arms comfortably at your sides, close your eyes and draw your focus to your breath, next visualize energy entering your feet and travelling up your legs and into the root chakra where the energy overflows and travels down your grounding cord at the base of the spine down into the center of the earth, allow this flow of energy to accompany the breath, next visualize energy entering your crown chakra and activating the crown, allow that energy to split into the two rear meridians and travel down to the root chakra, next direct that energy back up the front two meridians and out the crown chakra showering out in all directions and down your aura into the grounding, also allow this energy to split at the neck and travel down each arm and out the hands, allow the flow in the legs and upper body to naturally flow with the breath, maintain this visualization and focus on the breath for as long as possible, arriving at first light in the following morning gently bring yourself to an awareness of the room or your surroundings and open your eyes. Remember, this is a lifelong goal.

Next, we will discuss bringing healing to those around you and the planet. The great thing is that when the individual heals himself, he is healing the world at the same time by coming into a greater balance and coherency. There are numerous ways to bring healing to the planet, such as doing good deeds for your fellow citizens and planting trees, for example. We will focus on an earth healing meditation you can incorporate into your practice, as well as techniques for performing an energy healing session on someone who could use help with their healing journey. It is not necessary to become a specified healer, although the path of the Jedi Healer is a noble one.

Planetary Healing Meditation

Sit comfortably with your legs crossed and your back straight or on a chair or place of your choosing, gently close your eyes and begin to focus on your breath, focus on grounding yourself into your body and deep into the earth, next visualize a giant torus of energy flowing down from the high atmosphere into the top of your head and down through your body and into the center of the earth, visualize healing energy from the universe travelling through the torus and down through your body and down into the center of the earth, continue this for as long as you wish, then let the torus disappear and gently open your eyes.

Person To Person Healing Session

Have the person lie on a massage table, bed, or couch or sit on a cushion, focus on your breath, and grounding yourself into the earth; visualize energy entering your right hand and travelling up the arm; next, the energy travels straight down a meridian in line and perpendicular to the central meridian on the right hand side of the body and into the root chakra, next bring the energy up the central channel to the heart chakra and out the left shoulder and down the arm and out the hand, apply energy to the person's heart chakra to begin the healing, let your intuition guide you and apply energy to the areas you sense are in need of healing, apply to any blockages you sense, as well as specific areas you sense require healing energy, disconnect from the individual and clear your personal energies down into the earth, letting go of anything acquired during the session.

With these tools, you will build Force Awareness and eventually gain Force Abilities. Stay diligent with the practice, and you will see the results. Strong daily meditation and the practice of conscious rest will carry you through your ascension into interplanetary awareness and God's Consciousness. Exercises for healing others and the planet will increase your reciprocity with the universe and create more power for your Force Abilities.

You are well on your path as a young Jedi. Only the adversary of the Jedi path can stop your progress now, outside of limiting beliefs, although the daily practice will slowly purge all of those negative and limiting patterns from your mind. Ascension and adventure await, practice, practice, practice.

Fire Ceremony

A simple exercise but a powerful one. Taking a simple toothpick and blowing your negative emotions, such as your fear or trauma, into the toothpick and then burning it can be a powerful transformative tool. The witnessing of the emotion burning off in front of your eyes speaks to the subconscious mind. Build this ceremony into your daily practice.

Chapter 25: The Goal Of Emptiness

The Jedi finds peace in emptiness. At first, this may seem to contradict the seeking of enlightenment, but as you progress with your practice you will learn of great peace that can be found in emptying the mind. Emptiness is found through the process of letting go; the philosophy of meditation is to let it come, let it be, and let it go. This process brings one to a state of inner emptiness, which is talked about in Buddhism and Yoga. The letting go of all the material within the mind brings the individual to a profound state of oneness and emptiness, leaving only the light that permeates the inner dimensions. This state brings a profound sense of wholeness and liberation. The Jedi meditates on this inner emptiness and begins to know peace and equanimity. The practice of emptiness is central to the path of a Jedi, teaching the interconnection of all things. It allows the Jedi initiate to sense the illusory nature of the material world and begin to influence their surroundings. The loosening of your hold on the physical allows you to come into balance with the material world and then communicate more authentically with the physical. Creating the reciprocity necessary to move objects and feel energy. Through emptiness, the Jedi are free to use their abilities to cause a change in their environment. The following is a meditation to help strengthen your awareness of emptiness and bring about inner peace.

Emptiness Meditation

Sit comfortably in a place of your choosing, relax and gently close your eyes, focus on being grounded deeply into the earth and maintain awareness of the breath, allow your thoughts to come, let them be and simply let them go, allow all negative thoughts to pass and let go of any guilt or blame you are holding, allow the fears and judgment to pass from your mind while focusing on the breath bring your awareness to the empty landscape of your inner world, allow your awareness to rest in this emptiness, maintain a focus on the breath and simply let any thoughts that enter the mind to be and then pass from your awareness, maintain this meditation for as long as comfortable, then gently open your eyes.

Chapter 26: Plant Medicines & Intoxicant Training

Next, we will cover the topics of plant medicines and intoxicant training. Plant medicines are a very powerful healing tool; our planet offers a variety of medicines that the individual may encounter.

There is a growing movement towards legalization of psychedelic medicines across the world; cannabis becoming legal in Canada on the federal level and in most states, as medical or recreational, as well as in many other countries. Also, the legalization of other medicines, such as psilocybin and MDMA, as well as LSD and others. The Jedi can use these medicines to speed up their progression and healing.

These medicines can open pathways in the mind that will act as catalysts for spiritual growth and healing. The Jedi also practice something called intoxicant training, where a mind-altering chemical or substance is ingested, and the Jedi then mentally processes the intoxicant and works consciously to regain a state of mental coherency. These psychedelic medicines have a place within a Jedi's practice if used with caution and care. Using these substances comes with risks; the reader/student of this manual is expected to use great discretion when making the choice to use psychedelic assistants. Use with respect and use at your own risk; these medicines are not necessary for the path or for your progression. Allow yourself some time to do research and look into things before rushing down to the Amazon to take ayahuasca.

Start with the smoking of some low-strength cannabis that has some CBD balance to it at a low dose, and see how you feel; you may never need anything stronger than this. This will give you an idea as to whether or not you would want to take on anything stronger; cannabis can be quite powerful and psychedelic. Please do your best to observe the law within your area; the laws may be bogus and serve the elite control systems of this society, but they are not worth going to prison over. Taking a trip or relocating is a safer approach.

Cannabis

Cannabis can be a useful resource to The Jedi in training, Opening perception to the greater cosmos and building connectivity with all things. Cannabis is becoming more and more available as legalization continues around the world. If you find yourself within an area of legalization, you could incorporate cannabis as a plant medicine ceremonial practice, as well as intoxicant training, into your practice. The cannabis acts as the mind-altering agent the Jedi requires to alter consciousness, providing the test of regaining coherency throughout the intoxicant training session. Be careful with the dose, and start slow and low, starting with a puff and waiting several minutes before your next inhale.

This plant medicine has a lot to offer within the realm of intoxicant training. The individual can administer a small dose of cannabis and remain under the influence of this substance for up to six hours from one dose. Allowing the individual to smoke and begin with some meditation within the right set and setting to initiate a balanced experience, and then continue on for the next number of hours, consciously grounding themselves back into a state of complete coherency. Intoxicant training is useful to the aspiring Jedi's future; it allows The Jedi practice within the realm of being inebriated or out of balance, as could happen on the journey throughout the cosmos, as the Jedi encounters foreign gasses or atmospheres. Or while drinking water or eating food that is new to the body. A simple cannabis practice being added to your routine can prepare you for what is to come.

Start by visiting a dispensary or obtaining a medical prescription where available in your area; select a strain that appeals to you, maybe something of lower power to start. Next, find the proper quiet set and setting for you to initiate the experience. The following practice is a template for an intoxicant training session plant medicine ceremony.

Intoxicant Training Session: Cannabis Ceremony

Find a quiet place where you will not be disturbed, sit down comfortably with your legs crossed and your back straight or on a chair or place of your choosing; when you are ready to ingest the cannabis, close your eyes and feel all energies from people, places and things returning, ground yourself into your body and deep into the earth, next visualize energy entering your feet and travelling up your legs and into the root chakra where the energy overflows and travels down your grounding cord at the base of the spine down into the center of the earth. Allow this flow of energy to accompany the breath. Next, visualize energy entering your crown chakra and activating the crown; allow that energy to split into the two rear meridians and travel down to the root chakra. Next, direct that energy back up the front two meridians and out the crown chakra, showering out in all directions and down your aura into the grounding. Also, allow this energy to split at the neck and travel down each arm and out the hands; allow the flow in the legs and upper body to naturally flow with the breath; allow the energies of the cannabis to flow through the meridians and cleanse the body of any heavy energies, focus on the breath and continue for 30 to 60 minutes in meditation, gently open your eyes and continue from your place of meditation, grounding yourself into your body and deep into the earth letting go of the energies that have been brought to the conscious mind due to the ingested cannabis and come back to coherency throughout the following hours, carry on with your day refreshed and renewed.

This concludes what will be discussed in this book regarding intoxicant training and plant medicine therapy. Begin slow with plant medicines and intoxicant training; in another book, I plan on sharing more information on this subject, although it is a book within itself. Stay aware of your frequency of use when using these medicines, and have strong discipline when handling them, once per week at a maximum frequency, allowing time for integration; I recommend once per month. Respect the medicines, and have compassion for the trauma they bring to the surface. These medicines have very strong healing capabilities, as they uncover our hidden traumas and allow us to begin the integration process. Beware, you may uncover things about yourself that are quite painful. Keep a strong focus on your meditation practice throughout any plant medicine ceremonies or intoxicant training sessions, and in the time following, using the visualizations and meditations outlined in the previous text to ground yourself throughout the experience and afterward. Do the research for yourself before taking part in psychedelic therapy; there are numerous books you can find on the subject. In the future, I will be working on a manual specifically teaching the use of cannabis for a plant medicine and intoxicant training routine. Let the plants open your mind to the Force.

Chapter 27: The Lineage Of The Jedi

The great lineage of the Jedi awaits all who seek it. The student of this manual has all the teachings necessary to unlock this sacred initiation and progress on the path of ascension and immortality. The Jedi have always been there for us; they were with us in our ancient past, bringing the knowledge of the Jedi to the Egyptian priests and healers. They brought us their path of initiation and the wisdom to progress on the path of the Jedi. The early Egyptian priests adopted this sacred lineage and the title of "Jedi". We find ourselves through this sacred connection and lineage. It guides and protects us upon the path of ascension. This manual provides an initiation into this sacred and cosmic lineage, connecting the seeker with the ancient peoples of this planet and the Jedi who dwell beyond throughout the cosmos. Go forward with the teachings provided, and call upon these sacred masters to aid you in your progress. They will answer your call, as you are now a part of this great lineage of healers and warriors. The lineage of the Jedi is with you and will guide you every step forward upon this sacred path.

Lineage Of The Jedi Daily Initiation

Sit comfortably in a place of your choosing, gently close your eyes, next focus on the breath and grounding yourself into the body and deeply into the center of the earth, now visualize yourself on a mountaintop in a circle of ascended masters, also visualize a golden sphere in front of your body and a golden sphere behind your body, next visualize the ascended masters surrounding you, connecting with the two golden spheres, connecting with a vibrant green light from each of their heart chakras, now begin to bring the energy from the two golden spheres into your heart chakra, visualizing the energy entering the front and back of the heart chakra, continue the energy transfer for 15 to 30 minutes, then allow the connection to stop and the spheres to dissolve, now continue to meditate in silent presence focusing on the breath for 15 to 30 minutes, bring yourself back to your surroundings and gently open your eyes.

Chapter 28: The Path

Next for the reader/student of the manual comes the path, this is a lifelong eternal quest that may take you far from here. The universe is expansive, including the many galaxies and parallel universes talked about in the spiritual traditions of the ancients.

The journey will have its challenges, the biggest one being sustaining your meditation practice, although should you do so, you will achieve a state where meditation can rejuvenate your energy in a matter of moments, changing your whole experience of daily life. The student brings all of the practices of The Manual into their routine and gains mastery. The path will bring you face to face with the dark side of our society, and you will face them in order to ascend beyond the planet.

There are numerous accounts of people being taken off the planet with extraterrestrials; as your Force Awareness grows, you will begin to speak with these higher intelligence, and they will guide you and assist you with your goals of moving towards being interplanetary. Just because we don't see this commonly throughout our society doesn't make it an impossibility. People who claim to have been taken off planet, for the most part, have had the desire to return to this planet, so the extraterrestrials bring them back. There is nothing saying that when an individual reaches a certain point that, they could be ready to leave this planet behind and continue on their quest. Dream big!

From there, the hero explores the universe, looking for the secrets to immortality and the truth of who he/she really is on the cosmic level. Seeking to keep balance in the universe alongside the other ascended masters of the cosmic community. Looking for opportunities to find your way into the halls of all the great heroes who have come before you, the great Jedi lineage.

One day, maybe return to this planet to reflect on the incarnation and bring closure to it, moving on from there to plan your next incarnation and transcend to the world of spirit and the process of rebirth. Moving on through incarnations, gaining higher and higher levels of mastery of The Force, and ascension until the conclusion of the great hero's journey. This is the path of the Jedi, one of honour, and nobility. May you find peace in your quest, and may you achieve all your dreams and goals.

May The Force be with you.